Flops and Failures

By Steve Barlow and Steve Skidmore

WATTS BOOKS

© 1996 Steve Barlow and Steve Skidmore

Watts Books
96 Leonard Street
London EC2A 4RH

Franklin Watts
14 Mars Road
Lane Cove
NSW 2066

UK ISBN 0 7496 2034 X
Dewey Decimal Classification 032.02

10 9 8 7 6 5 4 3 2 1

A CIP catalogue record for this book is available from
the British Library.

Printed in the United Kingdom by the
Guernsey Press Company Ltd., Guernsey, Channel Islands.
Designed and typeset by the Harrington Consultancy Ltd
Karen House 1/11 Baches Street London N1 6DL

Contents

FOREWORD

Have you ever:

– Got Z double minus in a test or exam?
– Broken the family hi-fi by playing thrash metal too loud?
– Stood around waiting to be picked for a team until only you and the caretaker's dog were left (and then the dog got picked before you)?
– Called your teacher a pudding-faced dipstick while he or she was standing behind you?
– Been beaten at chess or draughts by your younger brother or sister?
– Been beaten at chess by your pet goldfish?!
– Been told that you're a total failure and will never amount to anything in life?

You have?

Well, don't worry! This book will make you feel a lot better. However much of a flopping failure you might think you are, there are people in every area of life who are MUCH worse!

Chapter One

SCREWY STARGAZERS

These days, we all know that the Earth moves round the Sun, and the Moon round the Earth. We know that the Sun is on the edge of a huge collection of stars, a galaxy, called the Milky Way. We know that the Earth is round and nothing falls off it because of gravity. Everyone (nearly) knows all this. But it wasn't always so ...

ARISTOTLE is considered to be one of the greatest-ever philosophers and scientists. He lived in Greece and Macedonia from 384 to 322 BC. At the age of 17, he went to Athens to study at Plato's academy. (Plato is also thought to have been one of the best, clever-clogs thinkers in history.) After Plato's death, Aristotle took his place as the Number One Egg Head and was appointed as tutor to the young Alexander the Great.

Aristotle wrote long works on practically every field of knowledge, including logic, metaphysics, ethics, politics, poetry, biology, zoology, physics and psychology! Hundreds of years later, in the Middle Ages, his work was rediscovered by Arab scholars and translated into Latin. His ideas formed the key part of university education in Europe from the thirteenth to the seventeenth centuries AD. In fact, his influence is still enormous today.

And yet your FOUL FACTS authors can reveal that

this Numero Uno, Big Cheese, Head Honcho, Top Man, total, class Know-it-All was a FLOP!

Proving our theory that, if you are going to be a flop and a failure, you may as well be a flopping failure on a grand scale, he was wrong, not about a silly little thing, but about a MEGA BIG one – the UNIVERSE. And you can't get much bigger than that.

Not only did he not believe in the existence of atoms (of which everything is made up); he also believed that the Earth was the centre of the Universe and that the Sun and Moon and planets revolved around it! He believed that this was all part of God's plan, and this was backed up by the Alexandrian astronomer, **Claudius Ptolemy**, in the second century AD.

Such ideas stuck. Aristotle lived 2,300 years ago. His ideas were still going strong 500 years ago. And they suited the **Catholic Church**, which believed that it was God's representative on Earth. Its leader, the Pope, said that he had a hot-line to God, so people had better listen to him or else. The Pope stated that the Earth was at the centre of the Universe. It had to be,

because God made it for Human Beings to live on, and Human Beings were the most important things in the Universe. (Next to God, and the Pope, of course.)

And then came **NICOLAS COPERNICUS** (Mikołaj Kopernik, to give him his Polish name), saying that Aristotle's theory was a load of gunk. He claimed that the SUN was at the centre of the Universe and the Earth moved around it. This theory was revolutionary. If the Earth wasn't at the centre, what was the Catholic Church going on about? And if the Church was wrong about this major thing, perhaps it might not be right about other things, either. Obviously, this was not good for the Church, which was very POWERFUL, very RICH and very DETERMINED to stay that way.

When people are wrong, they usually find that the best form of defence is attack. So the Church burned a few people at the stake, for opposing its view, just to let everyone know that it wasn't going to mess around.

FLOP, FAILURE OR GENIUS?
At the end of the sixteenth century, an Italian called Giordano Bruno believed that the Universe was made up of millions of planets and that the Earth was just one of them. Unfortunately, he didn't keep this idea to himself. The Catholic Church wasn't happy with people going around saying such things and after a seven-year trial, Bruno was burned at the stake. Right belief, wrong time to say it!

Copernicus avoided being burned, as he had the

good sense not to publish his theory until 1543, <u>after</u> he had died! He had set up a real debate. Lots of people suggested one or two additions. A Dane called Tycho Brahe said that the Sun <u>was</u> the centre of the Universe and the Earth <u>did</u> move around it, but all the other planets moved around the Earth! He obviously wanted to avoid the stake!

It was **GALILEO GALILEI** (1564-1642) from Italy who stated the what-is-now obvious: that Aristotle's view of the Universe was a FLOP! Galileo improved the telescope, which had just been invented, so that he was able to study the sky and observe that:

● The Moon reflected light.
● Jupiter had several planets orbiting it.
● The Milky Way was made up of millions of stars.
● The surface of the Sun had spots on it (which led him to deduce that the Earth revolves around the Sun).

This of course was BIG TROUBLE for the Catholic Church. The Pope and his Inquisitors asked Galileo nicely if he wouldn't mind recanting his teachings (that is, saying that he was totally wrong after all and that the Earth was the centre of the Universe) – or would he rather have an acupuncture session with some red-hot pokers? Being rather attached to his body, Galileo agreed to do what the Inquisition asked. Since he had been such a good chap, the Inquisitors let him off and merely placed him under house arrest for the rest of his life. Galileo's book was put on a list of prohibited books that Catholics were not allowed to read. It stayed on the list for 200 years!

> ## DID YOU KNOW?
> A Greek called Aristarchus, born around 300 BC, is believed to have been the first person to state that the Earth revolved around the Sun. Like Galileo long after him, he was threatened with punishment – in his case, by imprisonment – for teaching false beliefs.

ANOTHER ARISTOTLE FLOP

Aristotle said that heavy objects fell to Earth more quickly than light objects. Galileo proved that they fall at the same rate.

All stories have a happy ending and you'll be pleased to know that the Catholic Church finally admitted that Galileo was right and <u>it</u> was the flop and failure. It admitted that the Earth <u>does</u> move around the Sun. When? Unfortunately for Galileo, not officially until 1992!

PS There are still some people who believe that the Earth is at the centre of the Universe – and some who think that the Earth is flat! These are not only flops but also very sad people.

Chapter Two

LOUSY LEADERS
or "If I ruled the world ..."

Several people through history have wanted to rule
the world – or as much of it as they possibly could!
Of course, they eventually proved to be big-time
flops.

See if you can identify the following three
egomaniacs.

PERSON A – *Who was he?*
Born in 356 BC. Died of a fever in 323 BC.
Became King of Macedonia at the age of 20, when
his dad was assassinated. (Some people have
claimed that he helped organize the assassination.)
A military genius, but had a major ego (like most
military geniuses), and so devoted himself to
conquering the mighty Persian Empire and replacing
it with another empire ruled by himself! His army
travelled east, defeating everything in its path. The
Persians were beaten and the new empire was set up.
Still not satisfied, Person A ordered his army to go to
India and carry on conquering. However, the men
were fed up with all the fighting and told him to get
knotted: they wanted to go home. This annoyed
him, but he couldn't conquer the world all by
himself and so he was forced to turn back.
His empire fell apart very quickly after his death.

WHO WAS PERSON B?

Born 1889. Died 1945.

Wanted to be an artist, but could not get into an art school. Entered the world of German politics, but was arrested in Munich in 1923, after a failed attempt to seize power.

Became leader of Germany in 1933 and began a programme of terror which eventually led to World War II. Thinking he was a great military leader, he took personal responsibility for the war and the German army's disastrous invasion of Russia.

He thought he could rule the world and claimed that his third Reich would last a thousand years. It lasted 12. But in these years he had a profound effect on history and was responsible for the deaths of millions of people.

CAN YOU IDENTIFY PERSON C?

Born 1769. Died 1821.

A soldier from the age of 10, he became a brilliant leader who led the army of France to many stunning military victories.

However, his "I-want-to-rule-the-world" ego took over. He made himself Emperor of France and decided that he could beat anyone (or, rather, that his army could beat anyone, as he was only small and used to put his hand inside his shirt front). Person C tried invading Russia and caused the death of thousands. He finally realized that he wasn't so great, when his army was beaten at Waterloo.

Answers: A – Alexander the Great. B – Adolf Hitler. C – Napoleon Bonaparte.

Chapter Three

MANIC MONARCHS, ROPY ROYALS AND DESPICABLE DESPOTS

Looking back, it's easy to see which of the great rulers of the past were total flops, failures and dipsticks. The Romans produced gonzo emperors: for instance, Caligula, who made his favourite horse a senator, and Nero, who is said to have fiddled while Rome burned (though once the city was blazing, it probably wouldn't have made much difference if he had run about chucking buckets of water like everyone else).

However, some rulers were so amazingly useless that even people living *at the time* could see how terrible they were.

FLOP RATING * Pretty normal for a King or a Queen (or a Prince of Wales).

FLOP RATING ** Getting better (or, rather, worse).

FLOP RATING *** Pretty bad. Probably lost their thrones or their lives.

FLOP RATING **** Right Royal flops and failures.

FLOP RATING ***** Top-of-the-range, utter failures. If they hadn't been Kings, they would have ended up as beggars, thieves or quiz show hosts.

The FRENCH are acknowledged experts in producing Klutzy Kings. The most notable were:

Charles the Simple (AD 879-929)

Charles III was the son of Louis the Stammerer. When the Vikings invaded France, under their fierce chieftain Rollo (let's face it, anyone with a name like Rollo had BETTER be fierce, or he'd get the micky taken out of him something rotten), Charles followed a brilliant policy of giving them everything they asked for. This included the hand of his daughter in marriage and the region of Normandy. He would probably have given them the whole of France eventually, if his barons hadn't become completely fed up and chosen a new King, Robert. Shortly afterwards, the barons bunged Charles in a dungeon belonging to one Count Herbert (who we presume was as fierce as Rollo, if his name is anything to go by), and here Charles Simply died.

13

However, he may not have been so daft. The Vikings he allowed to settle in Normandy invaded England in 1066. They knocked spots off our lads at the Battle of Hastings, and seized the English throne

Oh, ReferEE!

(although an action replay showed that the bloke who shot King Harold in the eye was clearly a mile offside).
FLOP RATING *

Louis the Sluggard (AD 986-987)
Also known as "Louis the Idle" and "Lazy Louis", Louis V married Adelaide, which was ridiculous, as everybody knows that Adelaide is a city in Australia. His mother, Queen Emma, wanted him to form an alliance with King Otto (we're not making these names up, honestly!), but Louis couldn't be bothered. His mercifully short reign was marked by a serious lack of activity. He spent all his time eating and drinking too much before falling off his horse while out hunting – and serves him right!

He was so useless that, when he died, the French handed the Crown to another family entirely, rather

than risk having another lazy good-for-nothing like
Louis in charge.
FLOP RATING **

Louis the Quarreller (1289-1316)
Louis XI was famous for his stubborn nature and
bad temper. He married Margaret of Burgundy, but
presumably quarrelled with her as much as with
everyone else. When she was found guilty of being
unfaithful to him, Margaret was sent to prison,
where somebody strangled her. Overcome with
grief, Louis married someone else a few days later.

He sold land and titles to his chief barons and
bishops. The barons didn't read the small print,
because they couldn't read; and the bishops didn't,
because their minds were on higher things. Soon
they were all terribly upset to find that they'd been
conned into paying lots of dosh for completely
worthless documents.

Flops and Failures

It was rather a relief to the French that Louis was only King for two years before he got all steamed up playing a ball game, drank a lot of chilled wine to help him recover, and died of pneumonia.
FLOP RATING ***

Charles the Bad (1332-1387)

Charles II was King only of Navarre. It was his doing the dirty on his nearest and dearest, in an attempt to get his grubby hands on the French throne, that earned him his nickname.

Most people are quite happy with a set of glasses or a casserole when they get married, but Charles demanded that several bits of France should be given to him as a wedding prezzie, since they'd once belonged to his mum. King John II of France said, Sorry, he'd already given those bits to the Constable of France (this is a title of the French court, not some continental rozzer who says, "'Allo, 'allo, 'allo, what ees all zees, zen?"). No problem; Charles had the Constable bumped off, and went over to the English (who were at war with France at the time), so that John couldn't get at him.

Later, one of Charles' best buddies was Peter the Cruel of Castile (sounds a nice bloke), whom he helped to defeat the King of Aragon. But a few months after that, he helped the King of Aragon against Peter the Cruel – who, by then, was Peter the Absolutely Vicious.

Next, Charles' son (yet another Charles) had to admit publicly that his dad was a complete ratbag. Not only had he started plotting with England

again, but also he'd planned to poison the new King
of France, Charles V.

Charles the Bad was treacherously bad. And, in the
end, he lost all the territories he'd lied and swindled
throughout his life to hold on to. Which goes to
show that cheats never prosper*.
FLOP RATING **

Charles the Mad (1368-1422)

Charles VI was less fortunate than any of his
predecessors, as he wasn't weak, angry, cruel,
treacherous or stupid. He was just mad, which he
couldn't help. Sadly, you can't stop somebody being
King just because he's raving bonkers.

Charles was just a boy when he came to the throne
and, to begin with, he was quite a good King,
earning the nickname "Charles the Well Beloved".
Then, in 1392, he suffered a fit while riding in full
armour on a hot summer day. For the rest of his life
he suffered from bouts of madness lasting 3-9
months, with short bursts of sanity in between. The
French court, once the most flamboyant and
outrageous in Europe, became a shambles. When
Henry V of England won the Battle of Agincourt,
batty King Charles allowed him to marry his
daughter Catherine and made Henry heir to the
throne of France. This potty policy split France in
half, with the northern half under English control.

How mad was Charles ? Well …
He refused to travel by coach as he was convinced

* Unless they get away with it.

Flops and Failures

that his legs and bottom were made of glass and would shatter if he drove over a bump.

His wife, Isabeau, decided that it was too risky to sleep in the same bed as her deranged husband and so ordered her servant Odette de Champdrivers to swap clothes and sleep in the bed in her place. Charles never noticed the difference!

Various attempts were made to cure the King. One involved sawing little holes in his skull, to relieve pressure on his brain. Another time, some genius decided that a shock might be a cure. So ten men with blackened faces hid in Charles' room, jumped out at him and shouted Boo. Unsurprisingly, all this only made poor Charles worse.
FLOP RATING **

Other countries can't hold a candle to France when it comes to producing Silly Sovereigns, but there have been some good tries; for instance:

Ethelred the Unready (England) (968-1016)
The son of King Edgar, Ethelred came to the throne (a few minutes late) when his half-brother, King Edward the Martyr, died of falling over backwards onto lots of swords that some careless person had left lying about with their points sticking up. The finger of suspicion pointed at Ethelred, or would have done if anyone had fancied getting a finger chopped off.

Like Charles the Simple, Ethelred (or "Big Eth", as he was probably not affectionately known) tried to

buy off the Danes who were invading England and indulging in lots of pillage (whatever *that* is). This policy only made the Danes more greedy and they stepped up the pillaging. Wherever they turned up, Ethelred was never ready for them, and by the time he was ready, they'd gone somewhere else. To make matters worse, when Ethelred finally caught up with some Danish settlers in 1002, he rather tactlessly massacred them.

Ethelred's policy of alternately bribing and murdering the invaders was so unsuccessful that he had to run away to Normandy. Canute, the Danish chief, let him come back the following year, on condition that he (Canute) could be King next.

Unready to the last, Ethelred's dying words are reported* to have been, "Here, hang on a minute..."
FLOP RATING **

*Though not reliably.

Flops and Failures

Ferdinand the Inconstant (Portugal) (1345-1383)

Ferdinand I could never make his mind up about anything. He was betrothed to a Princess of Castile, but chucked her for a Portuguese noblewoman called Leonora. The King of Castile was pretty miffed about this, which was a pity as Ferdinand wanted to make an alliance with Castile against England. He'd already tried an alliance with England against Castile, but that hadn't worked out too well. Although he had brought an army from England to help him fight Castile, he had still managed to lose the war. What's more, he lost most of his navy during the fighting, and actually had to ask the King of Castile ever so nicely if he could borrow some ships to send the English army home again. After a career in which he changed his friends more often than his socks, Ferdinand married his daughter to the King of Castile. His annoyed subjects threw the entire royal family out and offered the throne to someone else.

FLOP RATING *

Ivan the Terrible (Russia) (1530-1584)

When he was just a little Czarevich, knee-high to an Iron Maiden, Ivan amused himself by throwing dogs off the palace roof to see if they went splat. At the age of 13, he had Prince Andrei Shuysy murdered by his dog-handlers. These were ways of rolling up his sleeves and spitting on his hands before getting down to some serious cruelty. When he became Czar, there was no stopping him.

He decided to rule one of his provinces personally, becoming, in effect, the chief gangster of the region.

He kicked out all the landowners and gave their property to his cronies. He evicted whole villages in the middle of winter – and in Russia, winter is WINTER. He had thousands of people executed; but he sent lots of money to monasteries so that the monks would pray for his victims' souls.

In 1570, Ivan led an army of 15,000 against the defenceless town of Novgorod. To keep his hand in, he had thousands of people slaughtered along the way and looted monasteries after beating up the monks. The massacres at Novgorod went on for five weeks and tens of thousands of people were killed. Many were burned, but most were dragged across the ice and tossed into a frozen river. It was a toss-up whether they died by drowning or freezing.

When he had time to see to smaller details, Ivan could be really inventive. His chancellor was hacked to death bit by bit, starting with his ear. The

Flops and Failures

Archbishop of Novgorod was sewn into a bearskin and hunted down by a pack of hounds. Ivan's treasurer was boiled to death in a cauldron (a clear case of cooking the books). Even Ivan's friends weren't safe: he forced one, Theodore Basmanov, to kill his own father; and then had him executed anyway. When Ivan's mother died of poisoning in 1583, there were mutterings (though not very loud ones) that Ivan himself was responsible; after all, he had killed his own son in a fit of insane rage in 1580.

His reign left Russia bankrupt and in chaos. The Czars of Russia were never able to recover the trust of their people; the hideous cruelty of Ivan the Terrible haunted Russia for centuries.
FLOP RATING ***

George IV (United Kingdom) (1762-1830) and Caroline of Brunswick (1768-1821)
Among the worst of our home-grown Ropy Royals was this obnoxious pair. George became Prince Regent in 1810 and King in 1820. He was a notorious gambler who rarely paid his debts, a liar, a womanizer, an over-dressed buffoon – and about as popular with the British public as a hedgehog in a balloon factory. So it says much for the powers of unpleasantness of Caroline, whom he married in 1795, that she soon became even more unpopular with the British government than her husband.

George only married her because Parliament agreed to write off his gambling debts of £630,000 (tens of millions in today's money) if he did. In fact, he had been secretly married already, but no matter: so had she. The first time George laid eyes on Caroline, he reeled out of the room screaming for brandy, and never left off drinking it until the wedding. This was because she was ugly (which she couldn't help) and smelly (which she probably could have). She was a coarse, cheerful, stout woman who went down in fashionable London society like a bucket of cold sick.

Caroline was bored in London, frequently remarking, "Mine Gott, dat is de dullest person Gott Almighty ever did born!" She sang incredibly badly. The Duchess of Devonshire, tapping her head, described Caroline as being "not quite right *there*". Immediately after the birth of her daughter Charlotte, Caroline went abroad where her scandalous behaviour was the talk of Europe. For instance, she appeared naked from the waist up, as "Venus", at a fancy-dress ball in Geneva (she was pushing 50 at the time).

When George came to the throne, he tried to divorce Caroline, but she wasn't having any of it. She wanted to be Queen Consort. By this time, George was so unpopular that even the dreadful Caroline found many supporters and her return to London sparked serious rioting. The divorce case was dropped, but not before a member of the government had summed up its feelings about Caroline in the following verse:

> *Most Gracious Queen, we Thee Implore*
> *To go away, and Sin no More;*
> *Or if that effort be too Great,*
> *To go away, at any Rate.*

The government, unable to bear the thought of Caroline as Queen, offered her £50,000 to go away, but instead she turned up at Westminster Abbey for the coronation. Although she was elderly and very fat by this time, she still had a habit of dressing as a little girl and this led many onlookers to suppose that she had arrived at the Abbey in her underwear. In best British tradition, the Abbey bouncers wouldn't let her in without a ticket, and the crowd jeered her. She died only two weeks later. This was suspiciously convenient, and it was rumoured that George had had her poisoned.

When George died, *The Times* reported, "There was never an individual less regretted by his fellow creatures than this deceased king."
FLOP RATING ***

24

FOUL FACTS QUIZTIME!

1

The Dauphin of France (a sort of French equivalent of the Prince of Wales) was to be married in Paris in 1770. Hundreds of French aristocrats had gathered for the wedding reception, which of course would be the Event of the Year, with a gigantic banquet and a ball followed by a stupendous firework display. Eagerly, the guests waited for the arrival of the Dauphin and his blushing bride. WHAT HAPPENED NEXT?

2

King Carlos I of Portugal was shot dead in the streets of Lisbon on 1 February 1908. Crown Prince Luis Philipe of Portugal was now King. WHAT HAPPENED NEXT?

3

Christina, the seventeenth-century Queen of Sweden, suffered from a fear of fleas. She wanted to get rid of them. WHAT HAPPENED NEXT?

ANSWERS

1 The fireworks intended to celebrate the wedding went off too soon. More than 800 people were killed.

2 Luis Philipe technically became King of Portugal – for twenty minutes. He was shot in the same attack as his dad!

3 She had a tiny 10-cm cannon made and spent hours firing miniature cannonballs at the fleas!

25

Chapter Four

MILITARY MUCK-UPS AND 'ORRIBLE OFFICERS

The Foul Fact about flopping military leaders is that their failures can lead to the deaths of hundreds of people (and not their own, unfortunately).

History has seen military muscle-heads sending men to their deaths, as a result of stupidity, insufficient planning and even diarrhoea! See for yourself with this chapter's selection of Deadly Failures.

General James Wilkinson (1757-1825)

This general was a businessman who made lots of dosh out of dodgy land deals and army contracts. He stayed safe and got fat while most of the real generals fought battles and got killed. In fact, by 1796, so many had got killed that Wilkinson, without having done any fighting at all, was suddenly the highest-ranking general in the US army. This was a problem for several reasons:

● Wilkinson hadn't a clue what real generals did.

● He had no idea how to run an army or fight a battle.

● He was actually a spy, for the Spanish government. They paid him $2,000 a year to keep the US army out of Mexico!

Wilkinson commanded an army for the first time at the Battle of Chrysler's Farm (1813), which he lost with ease. He found losing his next battle even easier. His army of 4,000 men was well stuffed by 200 British soldiers. By now the US military realized it had made a mistake and court-martialled Wilkinson. And yet the court didn't really see anything unusual in losing a battle in which they had had twenty soldiers for every one of the enemy's, and Wilkinson left the court with his head held high; not much of a trick as it hadn't any brains in it.

SIR WILLIAM ERSKINE

The Duke of Wellington appointed Sir William Erskine as a commander during the Peninsular War (1808-14). This was fought between the British and the French who were occupying Spain and Portugal. The problem was that Sir William was officially mad! He had been committed TWICE to an asylum for the insane, but was still considered fit enough to lead British troops against Napoleon! In addition, he had bad eyesight and, at the Battle of Sabugal in 1811, sent his troops in the wrong direction as he couldn't see the enemy!

Erskine was responsible for preventing the French army escaping from the besieged town of Almeida in Spain. He wrote out an order for his troops to guard an important bridge. Unfortunately, he put it in his pocket and forgot to give it to anyone. And so the French escaped over the bridge!

Finally he killed himself by jumping out of a window in Lisbon in 1813. As he lay dying on the ground, he asked bystanders: "Why did I do that?"

Flops and Failures

CHARGE!

Thanks to Alfred, Lord Tennyson's poem, *The Charge of the Light Brigade*, this event from the Crimean War (1854-56) has become known as something heroic. In reality it was a deadly failure.

The Crimean War was fought in Russia, near the city of Sevastopol. The opposing armies were the Russians and the allied powers of Turkey, France, Britain and Sardinia.

In 1854, the Russians attacked the British base at Balaclava. (Yes, correct! *That* balaclava! The hat was named after the place!) Lord Raglan, the British Commander, was sitting on top of a hill watching the British Heavy Brigade knock the stuffing out of the Russians.

He sent a letter to Lord Lucan, telling him to order the Light Brigade to help the Heavy Brigade.

Cavalry to advance and take advantage. They will be supported by the infantry which have been ordered to advance

Lord Raglan

Lucan was confused by this

message. Should he attack immediately or wait for the infantry? He made a decision not to make a decision and wait for some more orders.

Forty-five minutes later, Lord Raglan was a teensy-weensy bit annoyed that nothing had happened, and his temper wasn't helped by the sight of Russian soldiers dragging away some British guns they had captured. He sent Captain Nolan with another note telling Lucan to advance immediately and stop the enemy taking away the guns.

Unfortunately, Lucan couldn't see the guns. He didn't know where to attack. Instead of sending someone up the hill to have a look, he ordered Lord Cardigan to lead the Light Brigade towards the only guns he could see – which were the wrong ones. They belonged to the main Russian artillery. The Light Brigade charged. Nearly all of its 657 men were killed as the Russian cannons opened fire.

A French general was watching the charge from above. "It is magnificent," he said, "but it isn't war – it is stupidity!"

HOW TO TELL A LIGHT GUARD FROM A HEAVY GUARD

It was not really that the Heavy Brigade consisted of fat soldiers and the Light Brigade, of thin ones. A more obvious difference was that a Heavy guard wore a scarlet coat and a Light guard, a blue one.

ROBERT E. LEE (1807-1870)

Commander of the Confederate forces in the American Civil War (1861-65), Robert E. Lee was truly a great general, but even he made a foul decision at the Battle of Gettysburg in 1863. He ordered a massive attack on the Union position at Cemetery Ridge. He ignored warnings from his generals that it was an impossible task, claiming that his troops were invincible.

General Pickett therefore led 15,000 Confederate troops in a thousand-metre charge across open fields towards the Union troops and their artillery. Nearly 8,000 men died in this crazy attack – which changed the course of the Civil War.

Lee later took responsibility for the disaster (which was OK as long as you weren't one of the dead!) He claimed that he had been suffering from diarrhoea, which had affected his judgement.

Now to a Grade-A, Top-of-the-Class, 100%-Genuine flopping failure. The FOUL FACTS Most-Heroic-

and-Legendary-Person-Who-Should-Really-Be-Considered-A-Total-Failure Award goes to …

PA PA PAPAPA PA PAAAAAAAAAAAAAA!

GENERAL GEORGE ARMSTRONG CUSTER. You think he shouldn't be in a book about flops and failures? Well, we're afraid there is a BIG difference between the legend and the reality of George Custer!

THE LEGEND
- Custer was a superb general responsible for many victories against the North American Indian people.
- The Indian people feared but respected him as a great warrior.
- At the Battle of the Little Big Horn (25 June 1876), this golden-haired hero fought valiantly against thousands of Sioux and Cheyenne Indian warriors.
- Because of the overwhelming odds and the fact that the rest of the Seventh Cavalry didn't arrive in time, Custer and his men died in a heroic last stand under the flag of the Seventh Cavalry.

THE REALITY
- General Custer wasn't a general, he was a lieutenant-colonel. He used the rank of general to make him appear better than he was.
- He wasn't a good tactician – in his class at the military academy of West Point, he graduated 34th out of his class of 34!
- He was court-martialled in 1867 for being an inept commander, disobeying orders and

31

treating the men under his command cruelly.
- In 1868 he was responsible for the massacre of over a hundred Cheyenne, including women and children. The Indians gave him the name "Squaw-killer".
- He used the press to spread rumours against his enemies in the military and push his own case forward.
- It was his irresponsible behaviour and inept leadership that caused him and 212 of his men to die at the Battle of the Little Big Horn.

THE BATTLE OF THE LITTLE BIG HORN

Custer and his Seventh Cavalry were part of a mission to subdue the Sioux Indians in 1876. He was in charge of one of three columns, all heading towards the Indian tribes near the Little Big Horn River. General Terry, who was in charge of the whole force, told Custer not to act on his own. Another instruction was not to light campfires, which would give away their presence. Custer ignored both orders. Refusing to take any Gatling guns with him, he split his men into three commands and prepared to attack from the north, south and west.

There were 15,000 Indians gathered together, including 6,000 Sioux and Cheyenne warriors. They easily beat off the cavalry attacks from the south and the west. Meanwhile Custer was three miles away, trying to attack from the north. Imagine his surprise when Chief Crazy Horse and Chief Gall swept into view with thousands of warriors. Custer and his men dismounted and began to fight. His entire force was slaughtered. Custer's leadership was a complete failure.

And what about the final moments of the legend – Custer shooting at the advancing Indian warriors, his golden hair blowing in the breeze? It couldn't have happened. Before the battle, Custer had visited a barber's shop and had his head shaved!

The Legend   **The Reality**

A TRUER WORD ...

Custer looked down on the Sioux encampment and told his men: "Hold your horses boys. There's plenty down there for us all."

There certainly was ...

SOMME RIGHT IDIOTS

The Battle of the Somme, in north-west France, was one of the main battles of World War I – the "Great War", as it was known at the time. The Germans were fighting the Allied armies of France, Britain,

Flops and Failures

Russia, America, Holland and Belgium.
Until this war, cavalry charges and hand-to-hand
fighting had been the normal ways of battle. But
now these were replaced with something new:
trench warfare. The German and Allied Armies dug
miles of trenches facing each other, and protected
them with miles of barbed wire. Between the
trenches of the two sides lay No-Man's-Land.
Soldiers would fire at each other across it and
occasionally attempt to get across and seize the
enemy trenches. Such attacks were mainly
unsuccessful. Trench warfare led to the development
of certain nasty weapons including the tank and
poisonous gas.

Some British generals "masterminded" a British
attack on the German trenches at the Somme. Their
plan was for the British artillery to pound German
positions, kill their soldiers and cut through the
miles of barbed wire. Then 120,000 British troops
would advance across No-Man's-Land and capture
the destroyed German trenches.

But these generals were Deadly Flops and Failures.
The attack they had planned began on 1 July 1916,
and it all went horribly wrong.

SOMME FOUL FACTS
- The barrage did not cut the German wire.
- The German soldiers were not killed in the
  barrage. They took cover in deep trenches.
- The barrage ended ten minutes before the attack,
  giving the German soldiers time to resume their
  positions and set up their machine guns.

- As the British troops went over the top into No-Man's-Land, they were cut down in waves of bullets.
- By nightfall, there were 57,470 British casualties.
- 21,000 soldiers were killed, most in the first 30 minutes of the attack.
- The 10th West Yorks division was annihilated in less than a minute.
- Hardly any British troops made it to the German lines.

After this, the Battle of the Somme continued for five months, at the end of which the British had lost 420,000 men and the French, 194,000.

QUOTES OF THE DAY

Commander-in-Chief Haig called the Somme offensive of 1 July 1916 "the big push". In fact, it became the worst day in the history of the British army. Later, he summed up his day's "work", claiming that "The general situation was favourable."

"DON'T WORRY ABOUT IT!"

At 7.55 am on 7 December 1941, Japanese planes launched a surprise attack on the American Pacific Fleet in Pearl Harbor, Hawaii. Four hundred planes destroyed several American battleships and cruisers. The US lost 200 planes. 2,335 American servicemen and 68 civilians were killed.

The Americans could hardly have been less prepared for the attack. Although many US government officials in Washington believed that the

Japanese were about to declare war, they thought
that the attack would come in South East Asia, not
Honolulu. The 7 December 1941 was a Sunday. The
Japanese had predicted that the American officers of
the 96 warships would still be in bed, or relaxing on
shore – and they were right! Admiral Kimmel,
Commander-in-Chief of the Pacific fleet, was playing
golf!

As they weren't expecting trouble, the Americans
had left open an anti-submarine net across the
harbour entrance, and so several Japanese midget
submarines had no trouble in getting in.

So many American lives were lost because the attack
came "out of the blue". But, in fact, there HAD been
warning signs, which people either had not noticed,
or had noticed but ignored.

● In mid-November American spies in Japan
reported that Japanese warships were gathering
together.

- A huge Japanese armada was travelling across the Pacific, but no one spotted it.
- On 5 December the FBI tapped a phone call between Tokyo and a Japanese dentist living in Honolulu. The conversation was apparently about flowers – code for describing the ships in Pearl Harbor. The FBI didn't attach any importance to it.
- In the early morning of 7 December, an American radar station in northern Hawaii picked up several unexplained blips on the screen. The duty officer, Lieutenant Kermit Tyler (no relation to the frog), dismissed the idea that they could be Japanese planes. "Don't worry about it," he said!
- At 3.30 am a US minesweeper spotted Japanese submarines. Battle stations were called, but then called off.
- At 6.45 am a US destroyer spotted and sank a Japanese submarine in the harbour. It sent a message to headquarters. However, most of the men at HQ took an hour off for breakfast, between 7 and 8 am.
- And from 7.05 am, reports that the Japanese invasion fleet were headed towards Pearl Harbor were ignored because the wireless operators wanted to have breakfast!

Chapter Five

DODGY DEATHS

You may think that you are a flop or a failure, but at least you're still alive; and while you're alive, you can put things right, become a success, get the girl/boy/whatever, make your parents proud of you … For some people, by the time they find out what flops they are, it's too late – and so are they.

Wired Widdles

How can you be a flop by going for a wee? Joe O'Malley stopped for a widdle by the side of a New York subway railway line. He forgot that water is a conductor of electricity. When his urine hit the electrified third rail, 600 volts shot straight upstream and electrocuted him. A similar thing happened to an Australian, Sammy Bungan. He pointed

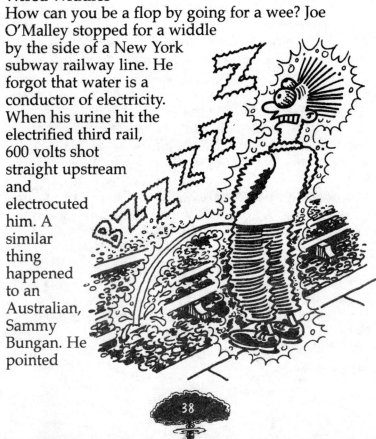

Percy and peed at an electricity pylon. He got the Power, and passed away.

ODD ONE OUT

Being trampled by elephants, chomped by crocodiles, gored by buffalo and mauled by lions, fair enough. People who mess with wild animals know what to expect. But some people are big enough flops to be done in by domestic animals. Who is the **Odd One Out** among the following? (You'll find the answer on page 45.)

Bradley J Bradley
King Alexander of Greece
Marc Quinquandon
Jerome Napoleon Bonaparte
Araldo Anastasi

DETERMINED DIERS

Most people try to avoid death, to the extent of hiding under the bed during a thunderstorm and not walking through Central Park in New York at night waving hundreds of dollar bills. Others seem determined to give the Grim Reaper as many chances as possible. Here's a gallery of them.

Zeuxis, a Greek artist in the fifth century BC, painted an ugly old woman. He laughed so hard at his picture that he burst a blood vessel and died.

Oliver of Malmesbury was an eleventh-century monk. He built himself a pair of wings, attached them to his arms and jumped off a high tower in an attempt to fly. He literally FLOPPED to the ground and was killed.

TWO FLOPPING PET-OWNERS

A man, who will remain anonymous, left his pet rat in a cardboard box outside Bristol Zoo, hoping that it would be taken care of, as it had become too big for him to look after. The local police smelt a rat (i.e. they were suspicious of the box). Thinking it might contain a bomb, they called in an army bomb disposal team who blew it up with the rat inside. And the name of the rat? – Lucky!

A woman in Durham in 1972 decided to clean out her pet canary, Beauty's cage – using a vacuum cleaner! She explained: "I switched it on and … whoosh! One minute Beauty was chirruping away and the next all I could see was a tuft sticking out of the nozzle."

Francis Bacon, the great seventeenth-century philosopher, failed with his final experiment. To test out his theory that ice would preserve things longer (i.e. deep freezing), he stuffed a dead goose with snow – then caught a cold and died of influenza.

James Douglas, Earl of Morton, was beheaded for treason in 1581 by a sort of guillotine called "The Maiden". It served him right since it was he who had introduced the Maiden into Scotland a few years earlier.

Karl Wilhelm Scheele was a Swedish chemist who discovered many elements and compounds. He, unwisely, could never resist tasting the stuff he produced. He actually survived tasting hydrogen cyanide (which became known as "Scheele's Acid"), but popped his clogs when he had a lick at a compound of mercury.

Peter Ilyich Tchaikovsy was a great composer, but he was a failure when it came to taking sensible precautions. During an outbreak of cholera in St Petersburg in 1893, he drank a glass of unboiled water, stating that he was less scared of cholera than any other illness. Oops, not a clever thing to do or say! He contracted cholera from the water and died. (Some people think Tchaikovsky deliberately drank the water to commit suicide.)

Arnold Bennett, the British novelist, certainly didn't intend to kill himself. He drank a glass of water in Paris to prove that it was safe. It wasn't.

Yousouf Ishmaelo was a famous Turkish wrestler, who made a lot of money from his fights. Afraid of thieves, he changed his winnings for gold coins which he kept in a belt around his waist. In 1898, the ship in which he was sailing home collided with another vessel and started to go down. Ishmaelo refused to take his belt off, and sank like a stone.

Anthony J Drexel III (what happened to the first two?) was a wealthy New Yorker. Showing some friends his latest collection of guns in 1893, he announced: "Here's one you haven't seen before." They certainly hadn't. The brainless Anthony waved the pistol in front of himself, pulled the trigger and became even more brainless.

Terry Kath was a member of the pop group Chicago. In 1978 he was fooling around with his new revolver, putting the gun to his head and pretending to play Russian Roulette. The others in the group

told him to stop messing about. Kath laughed:
"Don't worry, it's not loaded …". It was.

Reuben Tice, American wannabe inventor, was
killed in 1967 by a machine he was working on to
take the wrinkles out of prunes! This STUPID
invention exploded and Tice was killed in a trice as a
piece of metal struck him on the head.

Arthur Mandelko wasn't just your average
Superman fan: he believed he could do anything the
Man of Steel could do and annoyed his neighbours
by leaping about on their roofs. When he climbed
into his fridge, it was presumably to use his famous
heat-vision to escape. But the fridge
must have been lined with
Kryptonite
(or
something),
because he
was frozen
stiff as a
plank when
his
landlord
found him,
a month
later.

Flops and Failures

Langley Collyer was an American eccentric who lived with his brother Homer. They were terrified of burglars, so Langley set up an elaborate booby trap. No prizes for guessing what happened next: he tripped the burglar trap himself and was suffocated under piles of old newspapers and metal junk. Homer starved to death. The bodies weren't found for three weeks.

Mr Todd Missfield and **Ms Bonnie Johnson** died in 1974 when their Cessna airplane crashed into a roadside billboard in Canada. The writing on the billboard read: "Learn to Fly"!

A FLOP OF A HONEYMOON

A newly married Japanese couple were on a DC8 airliner that crashed at Tokyo airport on 4 March 1966. Sixty-four people were killed, but the honeymoon couple survived and were able to continue their journey on board a new plane eighteen hours later. This Boeing 707 took off and crashed. The couple were killed with 120 others.

How to be a flop at killing yourself

Vera Czermak, a Czech housewife, discovered that her husband was seeing another woman. She was so depressed about her husband's unfaithfulness that she decided to throw herself out of the window of her three-storey apartment in Prague. As she hurtled towards the ground, her husband just happened to be walking along the street below. Vera landed smack on top of Mr Czermak and killed him. She survived!

ODD ONE OUT ANSWERS

Marc Quinquandon is the odd one out. All the others were killed by their pets.

Bradley J Bradley was strangled to death by his pet orang-utan while he was sleeping.

King Alexander of Greece died from blood poisoning in 1920, after being bitten by his pet monkey!

Jerome Napoleon Bonaparte, taking his wife's dog for a walk in Central Park, New York, in 1945, tripped over the lead and died.

Flops and Failures

Araldo Anastasi's dog, Leo, was waiting at the window of a fourth-floor apartment for his master to return. In his excitement, Leo bounced about barking, fell out of the window and landed on top of Mr Anastasi, killing him instantly!

The odd one out, Marc Quinquandon, died of indigestion, after eating 72 snails in three minutes. This was a double failure, as only four months earlier he had become the World Snail-eating Champion by downing 144 snails in eleven and a half minutes.

Chapter Six

TROUBLESOME TRANSPORT

We tend to think that human beings are cleverer than animals because we can make ships, aeroplanes and so on. The truth is that we are only cleverer than animals when we make these wonderful things AND THEY WORK! Think about it. How many orang-utans went down with the *Titanic*? Well, there you are then. Here are some truly terrible transport failures.

THE *TITANIC*
The *Titanic* is probably the most famous ship in the world, but for the wrong reason. On its first voyage across the Atlantic in 1912, it hit an iceberg and sank. 1,523 people died.

The *Titanic* was the biggest and most luxurious cruise liner of the day. Its equipment and engines were the best that money could buy. It was supposed to be the safest liner in the world. Its designers had divided its 260-metre hull into 14 watertight sections. It was possible for up to four of these to be flooded and the ship still would not sink. Therefore the *Titanic* was advertised as unsinkable.

Diary of a Tragic Failure
10 April 1912: The *Titanic* departed from Southampton on its maiden voyage. Destination: New York.
14 April 1912: Ships in the area off Newfoundland

47

reported that there were large icebergs there, but the *Titanic*'s officers decided to sail on. At 11.40 pm the *Titanic* collided with an iceberg. The crew on the bridge thought that they had managed to miss it, but the sea was pouring in through a 90-metre gash below. The iceberg had cut through 5 sections of the hull. In less than three hours, the mighty "indestructible" ship went to the bottom of the Atlantic.

FOUL FACTS

1 There were 2,300 people on board the *Titanic*. It had only 20 lifeboats and emergency collapsible boats, with a total of 1,250 seats. (Only four of these boats were filled to capacity.)
2 The *Titanic* was travelling at 22 knots – a crazy speed considering that there were reports of icebergs.
3 The *Titanic*'s radio was not operating.
4 Another ship called the *Californian* was supposedly only 8 miles away from the *Titanic*. Its wireless operator was asleep and didn't hear the *Titanic*'s SOS.
5 A ship called the *Carpathia* was 60 miles away, but its wireless operator was not in the wireless room to hear the SOS.
6 The *Californian*'s crew didn't take any notice of the *Titanic*'s distress flares. They thought that a fireworks party was being held.
7 Many of the third-class passengers were kept below decks. 536 died, including 119 women and children.
8 Many of the crew were ordered to stay below decks rather than try to rescue themselves! 685 crew members lost their lives.

LOSS OF LIFE
Did it pay to be rich on the *Titanic*?

First-class passengers:

Died	Saved
119 men	54 men
11 women and children	145 women and children
TOTAL 130	TOTAL 199

Second-class passengers:

Died	Saved
142 men	15 men
24 women and children	104 women and children
TOTAL 166	TOTAL 119

Third-class passengers:

Died	Saved
417 men	69 men
119 women and children	105 women and children
TOTAL 536	TOTAL 174

Crew:

Died	Saved
682 men	194 men
3 women	20 women
TOTAL 685	TOTAL 214

49

Flops and Failures

The *MARY ROSE*

There wasn't actually anything wrong with the *Mary Rose*, Henry VIII's flagship. Sir Edward Howe, who led the fleet, described her as "the flower... of all ships that ever sailed", and she had a distinguished career for 35 years. Disaster struck in 1545, when the *Mary Rose* sailed from Portsmouth harbour to engage the French fleet.

The ship was overloaded, carrying nearly double the number of men she was designed to hold – extra soldiers and marines to repel a possible French invasion of the Isle of Wight. The best guess as to what went wrong is that all these people crowded on to the upper decks to see what was going on, be seasick, etc. This prevented the regular crew from doing their work and caused the ship to overbalance. King Henry and his court looked on in horror from Southsea, as his great flagship keeled over and sank. There were few survivors.

The remains of the ship were raised in 1982, and are now on display at Portsmouth.

SIX FLOATING FLOPS

The *Vasa* was a Swedish battleship which had grace, beauty and 64 guns. What it didn't have was ballast. In 1628, as the King of Sweden and admiring crowds looked on, the top-heavy *Vasa* on her maiden voyage was caught by a gust of wind, turned turtle and plunged to the bottom of Stockholm harbour.

HMS *Captain* was a British battleship that was virtually impregnable to enemy shelling, with all its

guns and thick armour. These made the *Captain* so heavy and sit so low in the water that in 1870 a storm off the coast of Spain sank her along with nearly 500 crew and her designer.

Why waste money on expensive shells when you can build a ship like the **USS *Katahdin*** (1893) with a big spike on the front to ram your opponent? Well, because it's an amazingly stupid idea, especially when, like the US Navy, you make the ship too slow to catch anything else that floats.

Believing that speed was a battleship's best defence, the British built **HMS *Invincible*** and **HMS *Hood*** with hulls like eggshells to make them light. Fast they were, but invincible they weren't. The *Invincible* was sunk by a single shell in 1916. So was the *Hood*, in 1941. The twenty-five years between the two just go to show that we British won't be panicked into changing a design that has turned out to be a dreadful mistake.

In 1967, on the way from Japan to America, the *Argo Merchant* suffered a collision, caught fire three times and had to stop for repairs five times. In the following year, the crew mutinied. After that, the ship ran aground off Borneo, and later off Sicily. She had to be towed into New York harbour when her engines failed – by which point a number of ports refused to allow the ship entry. In 1976, during her final hours, the *Argo Merchant*'s navigational equipment broke down. Her multinational crew were already finding communication among themselves a problem, and now they were

hopelessly lost as well. Following a display of seamanship that made Captain Pugwash look like Sir Francis Drake, the confused crew ran their cruddy craft aground off Cape Cod, causing an enormous oil slick. Finally, the wretched vessel sank.

... and TWO SUBMARINES THAT SUCKED

A French sub, *Le Plongeur* (1863) was fine on the surface, but a waste of space underwater. It would dive like a brick and then shoot up out of the water like a plastic duck. At least the French had the sense to scrap it before it killed everybody on board.

The **CSS** *Hunley* was really a ship's boiler cobbled into a sub by the Confederate navy in the American Civil War. There were no engines; the propeller was worked by eight men turning a crank. Torpedo technology being a bit primitive at the time, the sub attacked ships with a bomb on the end of a 4.5-metre stick. In 1864, after killing a number of men (including its inventor) in tests, the *Hunley* successfully blew up the Union ship *Housatonic*, blowing itself up at the same time. It went down with all hands.

PUTRID PLANES

If a car doesn't work, you can get out and push it. If a boat doesn't work, you can jump out and swim for it. An aeroplane had *better* work. However, not all of them did. Here are a few lame ducks among the eagles ...

The enormous *Batson Flying House* was built in 1913 for a planned trans-Atlantic flight. As it featured a sitting room and bedrooms for the crew in a gigantic fuselage, along with stumpy little wings and titchy engines, it never got off the ground, let alone above the sea.

The *Caproni Ca 90* had eight huge engines and so many wings it looked like a Venetian blind. On its test flight in 1921, the aircraft's designer, Count Caproni, had the fuselage loaded with sandbags to make the plane fly as though it were carrying 60 passengers. When the massive flying boat struggled into the air, it flew level for only a few seconds before going into a dive. All the sandbags tumbled into the nose, ripping off most of the wings and plunging the monstrous machine into the lake.

A PITIFUL PARACHUTE

A French inventor, Monsieur Franz Reichelt designed a clever combination of overcoat and parachute, in case you should feel like getting out of an aeroplane in wet weather. His invention was a terrific success, but only as an overcoat, as he found out (very briefly) by jumping off the top of the Eiffel Tower to his death in 1911.

The *Mitsubishi G4M ("Betty")* was a World War 2 Japanese heavy bomber. In order to increase the distance the aircraft could fly, the manufacturers removed nearly all its protective armour and installed huge fuel tanks. This meant that the aircraft would frequently blow up as soon as it was hit. Heartless American pilots referred to it as the "one shot lighter".

HOW NOT TO REFUEL

The Marquis De Pinedo was one of the first aviators to cross the South Atlantic. He travelled, in his flying boat the *Santa Maria*, from Italy to South America in an attempt to promote Mussolini's fascist government. But things went horribly wrong when De Pinedo made a refuelling stop in Arizona and dumped excess fuel in the lake. WHOOSH! The *Santa Maria* was burned to a crisp and the intrepid airman had to go home by sea.

CRUDDY CARS

The **Ford Edsel** was launched in 1957 and was meant to establish Ford's position as the leading motor-manufacturer in America. But this car was almost unbelievably naff. The name, for starters. The Ford *WHICH*? The Ford Mustang, yes; the Chevrolet Stingray, tasty; but the *Edsel*? A computer was programmed with marketing data to produce this name that would appeal to everybody!

The car itself was a flopping failure. It had loads of chrome and all sorts of gadgets, but none of them worked. Things fell off, doors refused to open or close, gearboxes ground to a halt and brakes didn't. The whole thing was about the weight of a small tank and guzzled fuel, just as petrol prices were going up and people wanted economical cars. There was only one good thing about owning an Edsel: at least nobody in their right mind would try to nick it.

The good old days of the Trebant. Until the collapse of Communism, East Germans wanting a car were only allowed to buy an ugly little model with a two-stroke engine called the Trebant. The car gave off its own private smoke screen as it dragged along at not much more than walking pace. Once the Berlin Wall came down, production of Trebants ceased, and people were allowed to buy Ladas and Skodas instead. Hurrah! But the latest news is that Trebants are making a come-back. People are feeling nostalgic for the good old days of long journeys and carbon monoxide poisoning.

THE FOUL FACTS MOST STUPID TRANSPORT FLOP AWARD

The award is given to the Sinclair C5. Anyone with the slightest sense should have realized that this was going to be a total flop. It was a mad little contraption launched in 1985 by Sir Clive Sinclair, to solve all London's traffic problems, presumably by wiping out all the people who were daft enough to try to get to work on one.

It looked like a streamlined go-kart and ran on batteries. You sat in it with your knees in the air and steered it with a bar that fitted underneath your knees. Nifty. All you had to do then was avoid getting smashed to a pulp by the millions of cars, buses and trucks that pour into London every day at speeds well above anything the C5 could manage. Average London drivers weren't about to give road space to a little motorized cartie, if they did happen to spot it – which wasn't easy, although later models of the C5 had a flag on a stick in a desperate attempt to make them more noticeable. In addition, C5 riders were just at a nice height to be gassed by car exhausts. Amazingly enough, the C5 never caught on.

Chapter Seven

MOVIES THAT MISSED BY MILES

The average success rate in Hollywood Movies is one golden goose to half a dozen turkeys. Some films turn out badly because their makers are several crowd scenes short of an epic; others, because they are made on tiny budgets. Some films have big budgets, great stars, brilliant directors – and still manage to end up playing to an audience of two usherettes and the projectionist's cat. Here is a selection of the finest box-office bombs in Hollywood's half-baked history.

A ONE-LINE PUT-DOWN
The trailer for the first *Alien* film said, "In space, no-one can hear you scream." Of *Alien 3* a critic wrote in the *Los Angeles Leader*: "In space, no-one can hear you snore."

INTOLERANCE (1916)
This was a silent film made by D.W. Griffiths. It tried to tell four similar stories from different historical periods, baffling audiences as the scene jumped from modern America to ancient Babylon to sixteenth-century France.

The huge stage for the Babylonian scenes, complete with life-size plaster elephants, was the biggest film

set ever built (it STILL holds the record!), but this wasn't enough for Griffiths. He hired real elephants to push the siege towers of the Persian army. Unfortunately, the male ones preferred to chase after the lady elephants!

The battle scenes were very realistic. Hundreds of Los Angeles mobsters and lowlife bums were employed as extras for the crowd scenes. Great! They could knock seven kinds of snot out of each other and get paid for it! In one day's filming, seventy members of the cast had to be given first aid.

In spite of such efforts, the film failed. One reason was that, a few weeks before it opened, America declared war on Germany. The film's be-nice-to-foreigners message wasn't what people wanted to hear any more. It cost about $2 million to produce – twenty times more expensive than any other film made at that time. Griffiths was ruined and banned from the studio for life.

NOAH'S ARK (1929)

This was another mishmash of biblical and modern stories, for which 7500 extras were sprayed with fruit juice to give them "authentic" skin colour (nobody ever explained how they knew it was "authentic"). It had a laughable script and a dim star (like many films since) and the *New Yorker* magazine decribed it as "... the worst picture ever made".

It was the making of the flood scene that really gave *Noah's Ark* a place in the annals of movie-making. The "Temple of Moloch" part of the set was filled with extras who had no idea what was going to happen. Then water from huge reservoirs was released suddenly towards them. The chief cameraman refused to shoot the scene, on humanitarian grounds, and walked off the picture, but the filming went ahead anyway. In the mayhem, six extras were crippled, another lost a leg and three were killed.

THE TERROR OF TINY TOWN (1938)

This tasteless Western musical consisted largely of people under 1.2 metres tall, riding the prairie on Shetland ponies and doing all the things regular Hollywood cowboys do. Even by Hollywood standards, this was one sick movie.

ROBOT MONSTER (1953)

Made on the sort of budget that a primary school spends on paper clips, this poverty-stricken science fiction movie couldn't actually afford a robot monster, so the Thing turns out to be a guy wearing a gorilla suit and a diving helmet. The writers never

seemed sure whether this monster came from the Moon or Mars, but everyone knows it went straight down the toilet.

UNDERWATER! (1955)

It wasn't only that the story *was* wet, and the actors *got* wet; even the audience was drenched in this fishy frolic. Aeroplane designer Howard Hughes produced the film, and invited 150 critics and reporters to the first showing. After three days of free drinks to ensure that they would be in good moods, they were each given an aqualung and guided (by a troop of "Usherwets") to benches anchored to the bottom of a lake in Florida where a screen and projector had been set up.

The pictures were pretty muzzy and nobody could hear the soundtrack underwater. Soon, the critics' enthusiasm was as damp as their goose-pimply bodies, and they headed back to the bar.

FOUL WORDS

Many critics panned *Star Wars* and its sequels when they came out. *The Empire Strikes Back* was described as "malodorous offal" (we think that's not particularly pleasant) ; and *R2D2* as an "oversized petrol pump".

THE CONQUEROR **(1956)**

In every film John Wayne ever made, he played John Wayne. This led to a famous incident during the making of *The Greatest Story Ever Told*. There was Christ on the cross, and Wayne, as the Centurion, had to say: "Truly, this man was the Son of God."

Take One:
Wayne: "Truly, this man was the Son of God."
Director: "Cut! Say it with awe, John."
Wayne: "OK."

Take Two:
Wayne: "Awwww, truly this man wuz the Sawn av Gawd."

With this sort of experience, Wayne was clearly just the right man to play the Mongolian emperor Genghis Khan in *The Conqueror* (if Mongolian emperors talked and walked like cowboys with piles). His co-star was an authentic Mongolian red-haired Irish actress called Susan Hayward. And to complete the realistic atmosphere, a bad-tempered panther which kept trying to eat Hayward was replaced by a toothless old mountain lion painted black.

Between them, the scriptwriter and Wayne produced many memorable lines. For example: "She is a wuhman-*much* wuhman!" and the immortal: "Yer beautiful in yer wrath!"

PROVERBIAL CRITICISM
The kindest thing the critics had to say about *The Conqueror* was: "It never Waynes but it bores."

Still, there are lots of bad movies about; what makes *The Conqueror* unique is that, unknown to anyone, atom-bomb testing in 1953 had turned the valley where the film was shot into a radioactive deathtrap. Over the following years, half the cast and crew, including Wayne, Hayward and director Dick Powell, died from cancer, probably as a result of their exposure to the radioactivity.

THE BIGGEST BOX-OFFICE BOMB

So far, the biggest failure of all is *Heaven's Gate*, directed by Michael Cimino in 1980. It cost $57 million to make, and took only $1.5 million in rentals in North America.

RAISE THE TITANIC (1980)

A British clunker, this. The story of the recovery of a secret weapon that went down with the *Titanic* is daft enough. But what makes this messy movie most memorable is the producers' expenditure of over $350,000 on a 15-metre model of the ship, without having checked that the studio tank was big enough to hold it. It wasn't, so rather than junk the model, the producers had a bigger tank built. *That* cost them $6 million. Sir Lew Grade, the head of the film company, later said that "it would have been cheaper to lower the Atlantic!"

YOU CAN'T WIN THEM ALL, RIK

One critic reported that *Drop Dead Fred* starring Rik Mayall had become popular in America, "… but then, so has serial killing". Another, for *The Scotsman,* said: "Mayall will empty cinemas; his performance is as funny as a kick in the pants." An American critic called the film "putrid … recommended only for people who think nose picking is funny".

Chapter Eight

PUTRID PERFORMERS AND SEEDY SHOWS

The theatre is famous for things going wrong. Most of us do daft things in front of our friends and families, but actors foul up in front of hundreds of complete strangers; and in the theatre, unlike in film or TV, you can't do it all over again and send the dodgy bit to a video clangers show. Here are some gruesome gaffes from the wacky world of showbiz.

A SHOWBIZ JOKE

Actors are notoriously jealous, so the joke goes:

Question: *How many actors does it take to change a lightbulb?*

Answer: *Twenty. One to swap the bulbs, and another nineteen to stand around saying, "That could have been me up there ..."*

Here Comes A Chopper ...

Robert Bolt's play *A Man for All Seasons* features the execution of its hero, Sir Thomas More. In a recent production, at the moment of the beheading, the block and the actor's head were supposed to move out of the way and a dummy head was meant to drop onto the stage. But in one performance the trick went wrong. The "executioner" couldn't see very well through his mask and cheerfully brought his axe whomping down.

Luckily for the actor playing Sir Thomas, the axe was a dummy made of wood. Nonetheless he ended up with several stitches, a headache, and a feeling that people who were beheaded probably didn't know much about it.

Making Waves

Spectacular theatrical effects were popular in Edwardian times. At London's Paragon Theatre the audience got more than they had bargained for. When a wave-making machine used during a storm scene broke down, the local fire brigade, plus pumps, was called in as an alternative. Nobody seemed to have considered that the fire brigade's pumps were likely to be more powerful than an itsy-bitsy wave machine. The audience and the orchestra were drenched.

Flops and Failures

There was no audience at the National Theatre, London, when it was discovered that the tank being used to float a full-sized cabin-cruiser for Alan Ayckbourn's play *Way Upstream* had sprung a leak. The resultant flooding caused widespread damage and the tank, which had cost a fortune in the first place, had to be replaced.

GETTING OUT OF TROUBLE

The phone rang as part of the play. A well-known actor picked up the receiver and realized that he had forgotten his lines. There was only one other actor on stage so the forgetful one mused a moment, handed the phone to the other man, said "It's for you," and walked off.

Getting it Right...

In a play called *A Sense of Freedom*, the main character has to get out of a straitjacket. The actor playing this role wanted to make it look convincing, so after rehearsals he asked a mate to strap him in so that he could find out what it felt like to try to wriggle free. His mate went off for a jar, promising to come back and see that his straitjacketed friend was all right. But a few drinks later the mate had forgotten all about it and went home to bed. That was on a Saturday night. The play's director found the infuriated actor, still wriggling, on Monday morning.

AN ACTOR WHO FAILED TO BE HIMSELF!

Charlie Chaplin entered a "Charlie Chaplin lookalike" competition in Monaco. He came third.

The Worst Actor of All Time

Many actors have had one or two failures, but this isn't enough to earn the title of "Worst Actor of All Time". For that, you have to be truly terrible in every single part you play. There is no doubt that this award belongs deservedly to Robert "Romeo" Coates. He was born in the West Indies, where his father owned a sugar plantation. He inherited the estate and moved to England in 1807.

Arriving in Bath in a carriage shaped like a seashell and sparkling with diamonds, Coates took the English Theatre by storm. His approach was unique. To begin with, he would rewrite Shakespeare whenever he felt like it. He would dress up like a Christmas tree and wear several kilogrammes of jewellery, no matter which part he was playing.

His greatest role was Romeo. The highlight of a ridiculous performance was his spirited attempt (not mentioned by Shakespeare) to break into Juliet's tomb with a crowbar. No one knows what he planned to do next, because at that point the audience rioted, bringing the play to a close. In later performances, he cut that episode, but spread a handkerchief out on the stage, to die on, so as to avoid getting his costume dirty.

Nothing would convince this great man that he was terrible. Managements refused to book him, other actors refused to appear with him without police protection, audiences threatened to lynch him, but he believed that everyone who dared to suggest that he couldn't act was just jealous. During one performance of a particularly tragic play, several members of the audience laughed so hard that they had to be treated by a doctor.

It was a sad day for the English Theatre when Coates' money finally ran out and he was forced to retire. He was knocked down and killed by a carriage at the age of 74.

If Music be the Food of Love...

There are great singers, and good singers, and lousy singers. Occasionally there is a singer who is so mind-numbingly terrible that he or she goes right through to the other side of bad and achieves a sort of greatness in reverse. Such a one was **Florence Foster Jenkins**.

For years, she had been convinced that she had a magnificent voice, but her family and friends managed to persuade her that the public was not ready to appreciate her art. They were kind enough not to mention that the only way to appreciate the Jenkins voice was to be stone-deaf, unconscious *and* out of earshot. However, when her father died and left her a fortune, there was no stopping Florence. While generations of the world's finest composers turned like gyroscopes in their graves, she murdered their music by singing it in rhythms, notes and keys they could not have imagined in their worst nightmares.

For years, this astonishing singer confined herself to select audiences of music-lovers, who couldn't believe what they were hearing and kept Florence to themselves as a sort of in-joke. Then, when she was well into her 70s, a car accident left her with a voice that could reach higher notes than she'd ever managed before. Determined to share her new good fortune with the world, she hired the huge and world-famous Carnegie Hall in New York.

A packed audience sat open-mouthed as she entered dressed as "the Angel of Inspiration", wearing enormous silver wings, to sing "Ave Maria". In a programme in which she changed costumes almost as often as she changed key, Jenkins appeared as "the Queen of the Night" from Mozart's *The Magic Flute*, and as a beautiful Señorita (the fact that she was pushing 80 didn't seem to worry her). In this costume she sang a show-stopping number during which she threw rose petals into the audience. It went down so well that she sent her accompanist into the audience to collect the petals, so that she could throw them all over again.

THE MOST REVOLTING ACT OF ALL TIME

The prize for this must surely go to Hadji Ali, who billed himself as "The Amazing Regurgitator". His act was simply to swallow small objects and then barf them up in the order suggested by his audience, which is a good trick if you can do it. This Prince of Puke had a grand finale guaranteed to bring the house down every night. While his assistant set up a small steel castle, the Wolfing Wizard would drink a gallon of water followed by a pint of paraffin. Accompanied by a roll on the drums, he would then call on Hughie and shoot a jet of paraffin through the air, setting fire to the castle. As the flames leapt up, he would cry Ralph again and send the gallon of water across to douse the flames.

STUPID STUNTS AND GROTTY GAGS

A "gag" is what stuntmen call all those mad things they do: falling off buildings, crashing cars, etc. Safety standards in film-making are usually high, so stuntmen standing in for film stars are not our subject here. It is the amateurs who have produced the most spectacular flops and failures.

Abraham Mulder

This great showman decided to take South Africa by storm with his daredevil high-diving act. The idea was that he would drench himself in petrol, set himself alight, and dive off a tall ladder into a tank of water to put himself out. Good, eh?

Unfortunately, when he tried it in front of a lot of journalists who had nothing better to do that day, he'd just struck a match when the ladder collapsed, dumping him on the grass. Howling, the great artiste performed the fastest limp in history and plunged into the water. When the flames were out, he emerged, and was just congratulating himself on getting only slightly crisped when the smouldering grass set fire to the petrol in his clothes for a second time.

Flops and Failures

OVER THE FALLS

Going over Niagara Falls used to hold great fascination for the sort of nutsoes who these days go in for things like bungee-jumping and nude hang-gliding. A number of people have successfully gone over the Falls and survived. Several more daredevils (i.e. maniacs) have successfully *gone over* the Falls, but ...

Charles Stephens tried it in 1920. To keep him upright in his barrel, he tied a steel anvil to his feet. He also strapped his right arm to the inside of the barrel so that he wouldn't be thrown around. Unfortunately, the anvil smashed through the bottom of the barrel, so that when it was found, his right arm was hanging in there. The rest of him wasn't.

George Stathakis went for the big splash in 1930. He was a mystic and trying to get publicity for a book no-one wanted to publish. Besides, he thought the stunt would give him an amazing out-of-body experience that he could write about afterwards (he took a notebook along to record his feelings). Sadly, his barrel got trapped behind the Falls, he didn't write a single note, and his out-of-body experience became permanent.

William Hill, Jr took the plunge in 1951. He was a game warden who was being investigated for diddling the parks authority out of hunting licence fees. A crowd of 200,000 people, including his mother, watched his attempt. He thought surrounding himself with fourteen truck inner tubes

held together with a net would enable him to
survive the drop. As it happened, he was wrong.

THE GREAT BULLET TRICK

Of course, the only sensible way to perform a death-
defying stunt is to make sure that someone else gets
to do the dangerous bit.

Unhappily, this was forgotten
by American illusionist
William Robinson (whose
stage name was Chung
Ling Soo), when staging
a risky trick in which
he was
supposed to
catch a rifle
bullet
between his teeth.
At the Wood Green
Empire in 1918, he caught
the bullet in his right
lung, and expired.

Obviously, where Robinson went wrong was in
catching the bullet himself while his assistant fired
the gun. A Ghanaian magician took this lesson to
heart. One part of his act consisted of shooting his
assistant and then bringing him back to life. The last
time he tried it, the *first* part of the trick went off
without a hitch ... Unfortunately, the *second* part ...
er ... didn't.

FOUL FACTS QUIZTIME!

1

John Warburton was a book collector in the early
eighteenth century. His fine collection included most
of the first editions of Shakespeare's first plays. One
day he went out, leaving his servant, Betsy Baker, in
charge of the house. WHAT HAPPENED NEXT?

2

Thomas Carlyle's massive book, *The History of the
French Revolution*, took him years to write. A maid
was cleaning up one day, and came across the only
manuscript of this great work.
WHAT HAPPENED NEXT?

3

A tired print-setter was laying out the Ten
Commandments for a 1631 edition of the Bible.
Hundreds of copies were printed.
WHAT HAPPENED NEXT?

ANSWERS

1 Betsy decided to make some pies. In those days, pie
bottoms were often made out of scrap card, and she saw
all these mouldy old books lying around ... When
Warburton returned, he found that some of his precious
collection was beneath some nice meat and potato pies.
The rest had been burned to cook them.

2 The maid decided she couldn't be doing with this great
pile of waste paper lying around and burned it.

3 It was discovered that the print setter had missed the
word "not" out of the Seventh Commandment, so that it
read: "Thou shalt commit adultery". The Church was
not amused and ordered the printers to recall every
single copy of the book and burn it.

74

Chapter Nine

BAD SPORTS

There is a saying that, in sporting contests, it "isn't the winning, but rather the taking part that counts". The people and teams in the following FOUL FACTS FLOPS AND FAILURES ROLL OF HONOUR probably wish they had never taken part! They'll lose their place in the record books, when even greater failures come along!

AMERICAN FOOTBALL
Cumberland University in Tennessee were beaten 222 – 0 by Georgia Tec from Atlanta in 1916.

BASKETBALL
The Yemen side of 1982 are the biggest International Failures of Basketball – so far! They were beaten by Iraq, 251- 33.

BOXING
In a 1946 contest, Ralph Walton was adjusting his gumshield when Al Coutre hit him and knocked him out. This fight, including the 10-second count, lasted 10.5 seconds.

But in 1947 Pat Brownson floored Mike Collins even more quickly. This boxing match was stopped after only 4 seconds!

CRICKET
Oxford University scored 12 in their first innings

against the MCC in 1877. Northamptonshire also scored 12 in a match against Gloucestershire in 1907. The lowest first class aggregate for both innings is a dismal 34 – scored by Border versus Natal in South Africa in 1959.

DRAUGHTS AND CHESS

Have you ever been beaten in 20 moves in draughts or checkmated in 4 moves in chess? If you have, consider yourself a flopping failure – both of these are the shortest games possible!

FIELD HOCKEY

The USA's men's team were beaten 24 – 1 by India at the 1932 Olympic Games. The England Ladies' team beat France 23 – 0 in 1923. And spare a thought for Wyside Ladies' team. In 1929 they were beaten 40 – 0 by Ross Ladies!

FOOTBALL

Bon Accord were beaten 36 – 0 by Arbroath in a Scottish Cup match in 1885. Seven other "goals" were disallowed for offside!

CHEATING HELPS!

In an attempt to improve their goal difference and gain promotion, Illinden FC of Yugoslavia beat their opponents 134 – 1. But perhaps the opponents, Mladost, weren't really flops, as they had been bribed to lose heavily!

England beat Ireland 13 – 0 in 1882 – when England

were half decent! You might also feel sorry for:

Eldon Sports reserves, beaten 49 – 0 by Drayton Grange Colts in 1988. (Even the goalkeeper scored!)

Courage Colts Under-14 side, beaten 59 – 1 by Midas FC Under-14s. The strange thing about this was that Courage scored the first goal!

THE FASTEST GOAL

Pat Kruse holds a real flop of a record. In a 1977 League match between Torquay and Cambridge United, he scored for Cambridge with a header, after only 6 seconds. So why is he considered a flop? He was playing for Torquay – his goal was the fastest own-goal ever recorded in a first class match!

GOLF

A woman player in 1912 took 166 shots at the short par-three 16th hole at Shawnee-on-Delaware course in Pennsylvania, USA. She hit the ball into a river and it floated off. She chased it in a boat and finally got to it a mile and a half downstream. On her way back to the hole, she had to play through a forest!

Flops and Failures

ICE HOCKEY

The biggest flops ever in a world championship
match were the players of New Zealand in 1987.
They lost 58 – 0 to Australia!

RUGBY LEAGUE

Swinton Park Rangers lost to Huddersfield, 119 – 2
in 1914.

RUGBY UNION

Hills Court schoolboys hold the unenviable record of
being beaten 214 – 0 by Radford School in 1886.

In Denmark, the men of Lindo scored a flopping nil
points while their opponents, Comet, scored 194!

Japan were stuffed by the New Zealand All Blacks in
the 1995 World Cup, 145 – 17.

SQUASH

The shortest ever championship match was over
very quickly. Lucy Soutter of Great Britain beat
Hugolein van Hoorn of the Netherlands 9-0, 9-0, 9-0.
The game took just 7.5 minutes to play!

Chapter Ten

HORRIBLE HEADLINES AND NEWSPAPER NASTIES

There is an art to writing newspaper headlines.
Some editors' attempts may remind the reader of
Leonardo (the Mutant Ninja Turtle, not the painter).
For instance, after headlines like these, the story can
only be a disappointment.

**Nudist welfare man's model wife fell for the Chinese
hypnotist from the Co-op bacon factory**
(The News of the World)

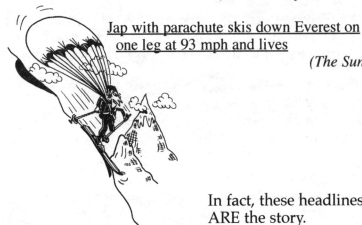

<u>Jap with parachute skis down Everest on
one leg at 93 mph and lives</u>
(The Sun)

In fact, these headlines
ARE the story.

Some headlines introduce the reader to a strange,
nightmare world:

SPARE OUR TREES – they break wind
(Evening Argus)

79

Flops and Failures

It's not much of a trick, but it's pretty good for a tree.

FARMER'S EIGHT HOUR VIGIL IN BOG

The poor man! Couldn't he have taken something for it? He puts us in mind of a little kid we read about in *The Evening Mail:*

"I am married to a sewage worker. My small son, aged four, pulls the chain after going to the toilet and announces with pride that it's on its way to Daddy."

Isn't that sweet? All together now: *Ahhhhhh!*

Decorating General Repair and Alterations
****

What about that Chimney Stack, Roof or
Gutter Job you were going to have done?
Don't forget that Paperhanging and Painting!

Why wait till Spring?
Don't kill your Husband!
We will do it for you.

NO JOB TOO SMALL!

Some headlines have a double meaning:

Super train talks

(The Guardian)

Of course it does, Mr Fat Controller. Just lie down. Doctor will be here in a minute.

Spotted man wanted for questioning
(Hackney Gazette)

Is that any spotted man, or do they want one in particular?

CRASH COURSES FOR PRIVATE PILOTS
(The Daily Telegraph)

Well, why not? Be prepared and all that. But what on Earth do these mean?:

Goldfish is saved from drowning *(The Times)*

SHELL FOUND ON BEACH *(Evening Argus)*

Gerraway! Did they find sand and seaweed, too?

WIDOW IN BED WITH A CASE OF SALMON, CITY COURT TOLD
(Liverpool Echo)

Well, some people just don't LIKE hot-water bottles.

Flops and Failures

DEADLINES

Headline writers and reporters seem to really let themselves go on the subject of death:

MAN FOUND DEAD IN GRAVEYARD

(The Evening Standard)

The Guardian reported: "Municipal undertakers have also gone on strike, but a burial ... was assured by a skeleton staff."

And *The West London Observer:* "At a meeting to discuss the route of a proposed ring road, the highways committee chairman said, 'We intend to take the road through the cemetery – provided we can get permission from the various bodies concerned.'"

TALES WITH TWISTS IN THEIR TAILS
Some newspaper stories seem to start quite
reasonably. You read them, you think, yes, that's
interesting, a bit dull but interesting, and then you
come across something that hits you like a stone in a
snowball. Here are four examples:

From *The New Zealand Herald:*
"Home Rule for South
The independent candidate for the Auckland
mayoralty, Mr P J Wedderspoon, issued a policy
statement yesterday in which he said he believed in
home rule for South Island.
He said his favourite pastime was standing on a
haystack abusing sheep."

Well, it may be ours too, but we don't tell the
newspapers about it!

From *The Birkenhead News:*
"Besides being the biggest bulk carrier to be
launched in this country, mv *Siglion* is also the
longest ship ever built at Laird's. Her length overall
is 820 feet.
The naming ceremony was carried out by Mrs Lill
Bull...and, despite her giant size, she moved
smoothly into the waiting waters of the Mersey."

Flops and Failures

From *The Daily Mail:*
"Paul Beard, 10, of Woking, Surrey, was rushed to hospital at Chertsey last night – to have a peanut vending machine removed."

From *The Daily Telegraph:*
"TRAIN HITS ARMCHAIR
A train from Ormskirk to Liverpool struck an armchair at Kirkdale, Lancs, last night. Later a train from Liverpool hit a pram in almost the same spot. No damage was done to the trains."

MEANINGFUL MISPRINT
From *The Guardian:*
"We find there are quite a lot of popils who come from junior schools who cannot spell properly…"

ADVERTISEMENT

CIVIL ENGINEERS (£2,277 – £4,143)
Applicants, preferably under 45, must be MICE with at least 3 years post-election experience.
(Sunday Times)

We have saved our two favourite items for last:

From *The Scotsman:*
"In the event of a nuclear war, children will be given a day off school, says the Scottish Home and Health Department."

From *The Evening News:*
THREE BATTERED IN FISH SHOP

Chapter Eleven

DID THEY REALLY SAY THAT?

Have you ever called your teacher all the rude names you could think of while he or she was standing right behind you without you knowing? Or made a confident prediction that has turned out to be wrong? You are in good company. All the people in this chapter must have blushed and wished they had "never said that".

"Can't act, can't sing, slightly bald, can dance a bit." This was the judgement passed on Fred Astaire, when he took a screen test to assess whether he had star potential. Of course, Astaire went on to become a Hollywood legend. Nothing more is known of the man who made that sweepingly wrong statement.

FAMOUS LAST WORDS

In 1976, the captain of a Canadian fishing trawler radioed to shore with the news of his crew's great catch.

"30,000 pounds – it's a record!" he announced.

Unfortunately, his boat could carry only 15,000 pounds and so it sank!

"Do what I say, not what I do"
British Transport Minister Ernest Marples coined the

phrase "Don't drink and drive" – but then didn't stick to the instruction. He was banned from driving in 1974 for driving under the influence of alcohol.

A nice welcome
On 22 November 1963, President John F Kennedy was visiting Dallas, Texas. He was greeted by John Connally, the governor of Texas, and his wife. As they drove through Dallas, Mrs Connally pointed at the cheering crowds and said to the President: "Well, Mr President, you can't say that the people of Dallas haven't given you a nice welcome." Later that day, Kennedy was assassinated.

WHAT THEY SAID AND WHAT ACTUALLY HAPPENED
These people got it horribly wrong:

The Shah of Iran, 1978: "Nobody can overthrow me."

The following year, a militant Islamic uprising led by Ayatollah Khomeini overthrew the Shah.

The Lord Mayor of London, 2 am on 13 September 1666 (on seeing a fire): "A woman might p*** it out."

The fire became the Great Fire of London. 13,000 houses, 87 churches and most of London's major buildings were destroyed.

Sir Richard Woolley, Royal Astronomer, in 1956: "Space travel is utter bilge."

Five years later, Yuri Gagarin became the first man in space.

Tommy Woodroffe, BBC Radio commentator for the 1938 FA Cup Final: "If there's a goal now, I'll eat my hat!"
There was and he did.

Phil Wrigley, a baseball club owner, about playing baseball at night under floodlights: "Its just a fad, a passing fancy."

It was a total success and remains the most important part of American baseball.

Sir Ernest Rutherford, in 1932, on his successful splitting of the atom: "The energy produced by the breaking down of the atom is a very small thing. Anyone who expects a source of energy from the transformation of these atoms is talking moonshine."

Rutherford's discovery led to the making of atomic bombs and the use of nuclear power.

The World Health Organization in May 1975, in announcing that it was cutting its anti-malaria campaign: "Malaria has been licked."

The same afternoon the Deputy General of the WHO was rushed to hospital suffering from ... Yup, you've guessed it ... malaria!

BIG-MOUTHED FLOPS
Some Big Mouths made the following statements
about people who they thought were destined to be
Flops.

1. "You will never amount to much."
2. "(He) would never make a success of anything."
3. "You care for nothing but shooting dogs and rat-
   catching, and you will be a disgrace to yourself
   and all your family."
4. "He is dull and inept."
5. "(He) lacks the big match temperament. He will
   never hold down a regular first team place in top
   class soccer."
6. "(He is only) fit food for powder" (i.e.
   gunpowder).

In fact, it was the people who made the statements
who were the Flops. They had misjudged:

James Watt – inventor of the steam engine.
Albert Einstein – the greatest thinker of the 20th
century.
Stanley Matthews – one of the world's greatest
footballers.
Charles Darwin – who wrote *The Origin of Species*,
putting forward a theory of evolution.
The Duke of Wellington – victor over Napoleon
and great British military leader (also became Prime
Minister).
Thomas Edison – inventor of the electric lightbulb
and the gramophone.

Can you match each of those famous people with the right one of the Big-Mouthed Flops' statements?

Chapter Twelve

FLOPPY PROPHECY OR HOW TO GET IT WRONG IN A BIG WAY

OK, you're getting towards the end of the book, but will you manage to read it before the end of the world happens? We hope so … as the world should last for a few million more years (as long as we don't destroy it ourselves). The Final Flops we are introducing to you are some who have claimed to know exactly when the end of the world would be.

FLOODIN' ECK

Johannes Stoeffler was a sixteenth-century German astrologer who claimed that the world would end in a giant flood on 24 February 1524. Thousands of German peasants took him at his word, built themselves wooden boats or "arks", and took them to the river Rhine where they prepared to survive the flood. Stoeffler was nearly right. There was an almighty storm and the Rhine was hit by a massive flood which drowned hundreds of the peasants in their arks. (Remember, they wouldn't have been there in the first place if Stoeffler hadn't predicted the end of the world!)

Despite the fact that the world continued on its merry way, a lot of people were impressed by this near miss and Stoeffler received great acclaim. He

lost it two years later, when he again predicted the end of the world and there wasn't even a shower!

THE FOUL FACTS AWARD FOR THE GREATEST FORECASTING FLOP

Is awarded to an American, Criswell. He or she doesn't seem to have a first name, but we know s/he is a former teacher (which probably explains a lot!) and claims an 86% success rate at predicting. These are some of the things Criswell has predicted:

1969 – *a brand new Korean War*
(Nope, sorry – not even close.)

1970 – *the assassination of Fidel Castro, leader of Cuba*
(He's still alive and kicking.)

1976 – *the devastation of Hawaii*
(Er, wrong again.)

1977 – *Black Death to kill millions of people*
(Sorry, no more than normal coughs and sneezes.)

1978 – *Lake Michigan to be drained*
(The fish are pleased to report that it's still full of water.)

1980 – *Cannibals roaming freely in Pennsylvania*
(Not yet been noticed.)

THE END OF THE WORLD IS NEXT WEEK, OR MAYBE THE WEEK AFTER OR MAYBE ...

American William Alexander Miller predicted that the world would end by fire on 3 April 1843. Thousands of people gathered on a hillside in New England on the appointed night, waiting ... Unfortunately for Miller and fortunately for the world, nothing happened.

Flops and Failures

Miller changed the date to 7 July. No luck with that one. So 21 March 1844 became the new appointed Date with Destiny. Again, nothing. Then 22 October. By 23 October Miller's followers realized that he wasn't such a hot shot at prediction and abandoned him.

WE HOPE HE IS A TOTAL FLOP ...

Perhaps the most famous prophet ever is the sixteenth-century Frenchman, Michel de Notredame, more commonly known as Nostradamus.

He wrote a series of over 900 predictions about the future of the world. The followers of Nostradamus claim that he predicted the Great Fire of London in 1666, the rise of both Napoleon and Adolf Hitler, the French Revolution and World War II.

However, we hope that Nostradamus is a total and utter flopping failure.

"Why?" we hear you ask.

Well, if he isn't a flop of a prophet, we are in BIG trouble. Nostradamus predicted that the world would be destroyed in 1999!

Keep your fingers crossed ...

INDEX

Flops and Failures

Flops and Failures